THE SWIFT ADVENTURE

A JOURNEY INTO IOS AND

macOS DEVELOPMENT

OLIVER LUCAS JR

TABLE OF CONTENTS

Chapter 1

1.1 Swift Basics: A Gentle Introduction
1.2 Setting Up Your Development Environment: Configuring Xcode for iOS and macOS
1.3 Your First Swift Program: A Simple Hello, World!

Chapter 2

2.1 Variables and Constants: The Building Blocks of Swift
2.2 Data Types: The Foundation of Swift
2.3 Operators and Expressions: The Building Blocks of Calculations

Chapter 3

3.1 Conditional Statements: Making Decisions in Swift
3.2 Loops: Repeating Actions
3.3 Switch Statements: A Versatile Control Flow Tool

Chapter 4

4.1 Defining Functions: Creating Reusable Code Blocks
4.2 Function Parameters and Return Values: Passing Data In and Out
4.3 Function Overloading and Default Parameters: Creating Flexible Functions

Chapter 5

5.1 Classes and Objects: The Building Blocks of Object-Oriented Programming
5.2 Properties and Methods: Defining Attributes and Behaviors of Objects
5.3 Inheritance and Polymorphism: Creating Class Hierarchies

Chapter 6

6.1 Optional Values: Handling the Absence of a Value

6.2 Optional Chaining: Safely Accessing Properties and Methods of Optionals

6.3 Error Handling: Managing Errors and Exceptions

Chapter 7

7.1 Arrays: Storing Ordered Collections of Values

7.2 Dictionaries: Storing Key-Value Pairs

7.3 Sets: Storing Unique Values

Chapter 8

8.1 The Basics of SwiftUI: A Declarative Approach to UI Design

8.2 Building User Interfaces: Creating Views, Text, Images, and Other UI Elements

8.3 Data Flow and State Management: Managing Data and Updating the UI

Chapter 9

9.1 Model-View-Controller (MVC) Design Pattern: Structuring Your App for Maintainability

9.2 Dependency Injection: Managing Dependencies Between Components

9.3 Testing Your App: Writing Unit and UI Tests

Chapter 10

10.1 Core Data: Storing and Managing Persistent Data

10.2 Networking: Making Network Requests and Handling Responses

10.3 Grand Central Dispatch and Operation Queues: Performing Asynchronous Tasks

Preface

Embarking on Your Swift Journey

Welcome to *The Swift Adventure: A Journey into iOS and macOS Development*. This book is your comprehensive guide to mastering Swift, Apple's powerful and intuitive programming language. Whether you're a seasoned developer or just starting your coding journey, this book is designed to equip you with the knowledge and skills you need to build amazing iOS and macOS applications.

Throughout this book, you'll explore the fundamental concepts of Swift programming, from basic syntax to advanced techniques. You'll learn how to create stunning user interfaces with SwiftUI, manage data efficiently, and build robust and scalable applications.

We've carefully crafted this book to be both informative and engaging. Each chapter is packed with clear explanations, practical examples, and hands-on exercises. By following the step-by-step instructions, you'll gain a deep understanding of Swift's capabilities and be able to apply them to your own projects.

As you progress through the book, you'll discover the joy of building innovative apps that can change the way people interact with technology. We encourage you to experiment, explore, and push the boundaries of what's possible with Swift.

So, let's embark on this exciting adventure together. Open your favorite code editor, fire up Xcode, and let's start building something amazing.

Chapter 1

Getting Started with Swift

1.1 Swift Basics: A Gentle Introduction

Imagine you're building a house. Before you start laying bricks and framing walls, you need to understand the basic tools, materials, and construction techniques. Similarly, before you dive into building complex iOS or macOS apps with Swift, you need to grasp the fundamental building blocks of this powerful programming language.

In this section, we'll cover the essential elements of Swift:

What is Swift? We'll introduce you to the core concepts of Swift, highlighting its safety, speed, and ease of use.

Getting Started with Xcode: We'll guide you through the process of setting up your development environment, from installing Xcode to creating your first Swift project.

Basic Syntax: We'll explore the syntax rules of Swift, including how to declare variables and constants, use data types, and write simple expressions.

Operators: We'll introduce you to the various operators in Swift, such as arithmetic, comparison, and logical operators, that you'll use to perform calculations and make decisions in your code.

Control Flow: We'll delve into the control flow statements that allow you to control the execution of your code, including `if-else` statements, `for` loops, and `while` loops.

Functions: We'll learn how to define and call functions, which are reusable blocks of code that can make your programs more modular and efficient.

By the end of this section, you'll have a solid understanding of the fundamental concepts of Swift. This knowledge will serve as the foundation for your future Swift programming endeavors.

1.2 Setting Up Your Development Environment: Configuring Xcode for iOS and macOS

To start your Swift programming journey, you'll need a powerful Integrated Development Environment (IDE) called Xcode. This toolset, provided by Apple, offers everything you need to write, debug, and build your apps.

Here's a step-by-step guide to setting up Xcode:

Download Xcode:

Visit the Apple App Store and search for "Xcode."

Download and install the latest version.

Launch Xcode:

Once installed, open Xcode.

Create a New Project:

Click on "Create a new Xcode project."

Choose a template based on your app type (e.g., Single View App, Game, etc.).

Fill in the project name, organization identifier, and other details.

Select the platforms you want to target (iOS, macOS, etc.).

Explore the Xcode Interface:

Navigator Area: Shows the project's files and folders.

Inspector Area: Provides details about the selected item.

Editor Area: Displays the source code.

Debug Area: Helps you debug your app.

Write Your First Swift Code:

Open a Swift file in the editor area.

Start typing your Swift code.

Xcode provides code completion, syntax highlighting, and other helpful features.

Key Tips for Effective Xcode Usage:

Use Shortcuts: Learn keyboard shortcuts to speed up your workflow.

Leverage Code Snippets: Use predefined code snippets to quickly insert common code patterns.

Customize Your Workspace: Adjust font size, theme, and other preferences to your liking.

Utilize the Debugger: Step through your code, inspect variables, and identify issues.

By following these steps and taking advantage of Xcode's powerful features, you'll be well-equipped to create amazing iOS and macOS apps.

1.3 Your First Swift Program: A Simple Hello, World!

Let's dive right into writing your first Swift program. We'll create a simple console application that prints the classic "Hello, world!" message to the console.

Here's the code:

Swift
print("Hello, world!")

To run this code in Xcode:

Create a New Playground:

Open Xcode and choose "File" -> "New" -> "Playground."

Select "iOS" or "macOS" as the platform.

Choose a suitable name for your playground.

Write the Code:

In the playground's editor, type the `print("Hello, world!")` line.

Run the Code:

Click the "Run" button in the top right corner of the playground.

You should see the "Hello, world!" message printed in the results area.

Breaking Down the Code:

`print()`: This is a built-in function in Swift that displays the specified value to the console.

`"Hello, world!"`: This is a string literal, representing a sequence of characters enclosed in double quotes.

Congratulations, you've written and run your first Swift program!

In the next sections, we'll delve deeper into Swift's syntax, data types, and control flow.

Chapter 2

Swift's Core Concepts

2.1 Variables and Constants: The Building Blocks of Swift

In Swift, variables and constants are used to store values. Think of them as containers that hold data.

Constants

Declared using the `let` keyword.

Their values cannot be changed once assigned.

Useful for values that remain fixed throughout your program.

Example:

```
Swift
let pi = 3.14159
let greeting = "Hello, Swift!"
```

Variables

Declared using the `var` keyword.

Their values can be changed during the program's execution.

Useful for values that need to be updated or modified.

Example:

```
Swift
var age = 25
var name = "Alice"
```

Data Types:

Swift is a strongly typed language, meaning that every variable and constant must have a specific data type. Here are some common data types:

Integer: `Int` (e.g., 42, -10)

Floating-Point Number: `Double` (e.g., 3.14159), `Float` (less precise)

String: `String` (e.g., "Hello, world!")

Boolean: `Bool` (e.g., `true`, `false`)

Type Inference:

Swift often infers the data type of a variable or constant based on the value you assign to it. For example:

```
Swift
let inferredInteger = 42 // Inferred as Int
let inferredString = "Hello" // Inferred as String
```

By understanding variables and constants, you'll be able to store and manipulate data effectively in your Swift programs.

2.2 Data Types: The Foundation of Swift

Data types define the kind of data a variable or constant can hold. Swift is a strongly typed language, which means that you must declare the data type of a variable or constant before using it.

Here are some common data types in Swift:

Integer:

Int: Represents integer numbers (whole numbers) like 42, -10, 0.

UInt: Represents unsigned integer numbers (non-negative whole numbers) like 0, 1, 2.

Int8, Int16, Int32, Int64: Represent integer numbers of specific bit widths.

UInt8, UInt16, UInt32, UInt64: Represent unsigned integer numbers of specific bit widths.

Floating-Point Number:

Double: Represents double-precision floating-point numbers with a wide range and precision.

Float: Represents single-precision floating-point numbers with a smaller range and precision.

Boolean:

Bool: Represents logical values, either `true` or `false`.

String:

String: Represents a sequence of characters, enclosed in double quotes.

Character:

Character: Represents a single character, enclosed in single quotes.

Optional:

Optional<T>: Represents a value that may or may not be present. It can be either a value of type T or nil.

Type Inference:

Swift often infers the data type of a variable or constant based on the value you assign to it. For example:

```Swift
let age = 30 // Inferred as Int
let pi = 3.14159 // Inferred as Double
let isStudent = true // Inferred as Bool
```

Type Casting:

You can convert a value from one data type to another using type casting. For example:

```Swift
let integerValue = 42
let doubleValue = Double(integerValue) // Convert to Double
```

By understanding data types, you can write more precise and efficient Swift code.

2.3 Operators and Expressions: The Building Blocks of Calculations

Operators are symbols that perform specific operations on values. Expressions combine operators and values to produce a result.

Arithmetic Operators:

Addition: +

Subtraction: -

Multiplication: *

Division: /

Modulo: % (remainder after division)

Example:

Swift
let result = (10 + 5) * 2

Comparison Operators:

Equal to: ==

Not equal to: !=

Greater than: >

Less than: <

Greater than or equal to: >=

Less than or equal to: <=

Example:[1]

Swift
let isGreaterThan = 10 > 5 // isGreaterThan is true

Logical Operators:

Logical AND: && (both conditions must be true)

Logical OR: || (at least one condition must be true)

Logical NOT: ! (negates a condition)

Example:

Swift
let isAdult = age >= 18 && isCitizen == true

Compound Assignment Operators:

Add and assign: +=

Subtract and assign: -=

Multiply and assign: *=

Divide and assign: /=

Modulo and assign: %=

Example:

Swift
var counter = 0
counter += 1 // Increment counter by 1

By understanding operators and expressions, you can perform complex calculations and make decisions in your Swift code.

Chapter 3

Control Flow

3.1 Conditional Statements: Making Decisions in Swift

Conditional statements allow you to execute different code blocks based on specific conditions. This enables your program to make decisions and respond to different inputs or situations.

if Statement:

```swift
Swift
if condition {
    // Code to execute if the condition is true
}
```

Example:

```swift
Swift
let age = 25

if age >= 18 {
    print("You are an adult.")
}
```

if-else Statement:

```swift
Swift
if condition {
    // Code to execute if the condition is true
} else {
```

```
    // Code to execute if the condition is false
}
```

Example:

```swift
Swift
let isRaining = true

if isRaining {
    print("Bring an umbrella.")
} else {
    print("Enjoy the sunny day.")
}
```

if-else-if Chain:

```swift
Swift
if condition1 {
    // Code to execute if condition1 is true
} else if condition2 {
    // Code to execute if condition1 is false and condition2 is true
} else {
    // Code to execute if neither condition1 nor condition2 is true
}
```

Example:

```swift
Swift
let score = 85

if score >= 90 {
    print("Excellent!")
} else if score >= 80 {
    print("Very good!")
```

```
} else {
    print("Good job!")
}
```

By using conditional statements, you can create dynamic and responsive programs that can adapt to different inputs and situations.

3.2 Loops: Repeating Actions

Loops are a powerful tool in programming that allow you to execute a block of code multiple times. Swift provides two main types of loops: for loops and while loops.

For Loops:

A for loop is used to iterate over a sequence of values. It's commonly used to iterate over arrays, dictionaries, ranges, or any other sequence that conforms to the Sequence protocol.

Swift
```
for item in sequence {
    // Code to execute for each item
}
```

Example:

Swift
```
let numbers = [1, 2, 3, 4, 5]

for number in numbers {
    print(number)
}
```

While Loops:

A `while` loop repeatedly executes a block of code as long as a certain condition is true.

Swift
```
while condition {
    // Code to execute while the condition is true
}
```

Example:

Swift
```
var count = 0

while count < 5 {
    print("Count: \(count)")
    count += 1
}
```

Important Considerations:

Infinite Loops: Be careful not to create infinite loops, where the condition never becomes false. This can cause your program to run indefinitely.

Breaking Out of a Loop: Use the `break` keyword to exit a loop early.

Skipping an Iteration: Use the `continue` keyword to skip the current iteration and move to the next one.

By effectively using loops, you can automate repetitive tasks and write more concise and efficient code.

3.3 Switch Statements: A Versatile Control Flow Tool

A `switch` statement provides a concise way to handle multiple possible values of a single expression. It's often used as an alternative to multiple `if-else` statements, especially when you need to check for a large number of cases.

Basic Syntax:

```swift
Swift
switch expression {
case value1:
    // Code to execute if expression matches value1
case value2, value3:
    // Code to execute if expression matches value2 or value3
default:
    // Code to execute if no case matches
}
```

Example:

```swift
Swift
let dayOfWeek = 3

switch dayOfWeek {
case 1:
    print("Monday")
case 2:
    print("Tuesday")
case 3:
    print("Wednesday")
case 4:
    print("Thursday")
```

```
case 5:
    print("Friday")
case 6, 7:
    print("Weekend!")
default:
    print("Invalid day")
}
```

Key Points:

The `switch` statement evaluates the `expression` and compares it to each `case` label.

If a match is found, the corresponding code block is executed.

The `default` case is optional and is executed if no other case matches.

You can combine multiple cases using commas.

The `where` clause can be used to add additional conditions to a case.

Example with `where` clause:

Swift
```
let number = 15

switch number {
case let x where x % 2 == 0:
    print("\(x) is even.")
default:
    print("\(number) is odd.")
}
```

By using `switch` statements, you can write more concise and readable code, especially when dealing with multiple possible values.

Chapter 4

Functions

4.1 Defining Functions: Creating Reusable Code Blocks

Functions are blocks of code that perform a specific task. They help you organize your code, make it more readable, and avoid code duplication.

Basic Syntax:

```swift
Swift
func functionName(parameterName: parameterType) -> returnType {
   // Function body
}
```

Explanation:

`func`: Keyword to declare a function.

`functionName`: The name of the function.

`parameterName: parameterType`: Optional parameters and their data types.

`returnType`: Optional return type of the function.

`Function body`: The code that the function executes.

Example:

```swift
Swift
func greet(name: String) -> String {
    return "Hello, \(name)!"
}

let greetingMessage = greet(name: "Alice")
print(greetingMessage) // Output: Hello, Alice!
```

Function Parameters:

Required Parameters: Must be provided when calling the function.

Optional Parameters: Can be omitted when calling the function.

Default Parameter Values: Can be assigned default values.

Example:

```swift
Swift
func greet(name: String, lastName: String = "Doe") -> String {
    return "Hello, \(name) \(lastName)!"
}

let greeting1 = greet(name: "Bob") // Output: Hello, Bob Doe!
let greeting2 = greet(name: "Charlie", lastName: "Brown") // Output: Hello, Charlie Brown!
```

Return Values:

Functions can return values using the `return` keyword.

The return type is specified after the parameter list.

If a function doesn't explicitly return a value, it implicitly returns `Void`.

By effectively using functions, you can break down complex problems into smaller, more manageable parts, improve code readability, and promote code reuse.

4.2 Function Parameters and Return Values: Passing Data In and Out

Functions can accept input values, known as parameters, and can also return output values.

Parameters:

Required Parameters: Must be provided when calling the function.

Optional Parameters: Can be omitted when calling the function. They are marked with a ? after the parameter type.

Default Parameter Values: Can be assigned default values if no value is provided.

Example:

```
Swift
func greet(name: String, lastName: String? = nil) -> String {
   if let lastName = lastName {
      return "Hello, \(name) \(lastName)!"
   } else {
      return "Hello, \(name)!"
   }
}

let greeting1 = greet(name: "Alice") // Output: Hello, Alice!
```

let greeting2 = greet(name: "Bob", lastName: "Smith") // Output: Hello, Bob Smith!

Return Values:

A function can return a value using the `return` keyword.

The return type is specified after the parameter list.

If a function doesn't explicitly return a value, it implicitly returns `Void`.

Example:

```Swift
func add(number1: Int, number2: Int) -> Int {
    return number1 + number2
}

let sum = add(number1: 5, number2: 3)
print(sum) // Output: 8
```

By understanding parameters and return values, you can create versatile functions that can perform various tasks and interact with other parts of your program.

4.3 Function Overloading and Default Parameters: Creating Flexible Functions

Swift allows you to create multiple functions with the same name but different parameter lists. This is called function overloading. It enables you to define functions that can handle different input types or numbers of arguments.

Function Overloading:

```swift
Swift
func greet(name: String) {
   print("Hello, \(name)!")
}

func greet(firstName: String, lastName: String) {
   print("Hello, \(firstName) \(lastName)!")
}
```

Default Parameters:

You can assign default values to function parameters, making them optional. This allows you to call the function with fewer arguments.

```swift
Swift
func greet(name: String, greetingMessage: String = "Hello") {
   print("\(greetingMessage), \(name)!")
}

greet(name: "Alice") // Output: Hello, Alice!
greet(name: "Bob", greetingMessage: "Hi") // Output: Hi, Bob!
```

Key Points:

Function overloading is based on the number and types of parameters.

Default parameters provide flexibility in function calls.

Use function overloading and default parameters judiciously to avoid confusion and maintain code readability.

By effectively using function overloading and default parameters, you can create more flexible and reusable functions that adapt to different situations.

Chapter 5

Object-Oriented Programming

5.1 Classes and Objects: The Building Blocks of Object-Oriented Programming

Object-oriented programming (OOP) is a programming paradigm that revolves around the concept of objects.[1] Objects are instances of classes, which[2] define the properties and behaviors of those objects.

Classes:

A class is a blueprint for creating objects. It defines the properties (data) and methods (functions) that objects of that class will have.

Example:

```swift
Swift
class Car {
    var make: String
    var model: String
    var year: Int

    func startEngine() {
        print("Engine started.")
    }

    func stopEngine() {
        print("Engine stopped.")
    }
}
```

Objects:

An object is an instance of a class. It has its own set of properties and can perform the methods defined by the class.

Example:

```
Swift
let myCar = Car()
myCar.make = "Toyota"
myCar.model = "Camry"
myCar.year = 2023

myCar.startEngine()
```

Key Concepts:

Properties: Data associated with an object.

Methods: Functions that define the behavior of an object.

Instance Properties: Properties that belong to individual instances of a class.

Type Properties: Properties that belong to the class itself and are shared by all instances.

Instance Methods: Methods that operate on instance properties.

Type Methods: Methods that operate on type properties.

By understanding classes and objects, you can create well-structured, modular, and reusable code in Swift.

5.2 Properties and Methods: Defining Attributes and Behaviors of Objects

Properties

Properties define the characteristics or attributes of an object. They can be either stored properties or computed properties.

Stored Properties:

Store values directly.

Can be declared with or without initial values.

```Swift
class Person {
    var name: String
    var age: Int

    init(name: String, age: Int) {
        self.name = name
        self.age = age
    }
}
```

Computed Properties:
Calculate a value based on other properties or external factors.
Can be read-only or read-write.

```swift
Swift
class Circle {
    var radius: Double

    var diameter: Double {
        get {
            return radius * 2
        }
        set {
            radius = newValue / 2
        }
    }
}
```

Methods

Methods define the actions or behaviors that an object can perform. They can be instance methods or type methods.

Instance Methods:

Operate on instance properties.

Can modify the state of the object.

```swift
Swift
class Person {
    // ...

    func greet() {
        print("Hello, my name is \(name).")
    }
}
```

Type Methods:

Operate on type properties.

Can be used to create utility functions related to the class.

Swift
```
class Circle {
    // ...

    class func calculateArea(radius: Double) -> Double {
        return Double.pi * radius * radius
    }
}
```

By effectively using properties and methods, you can create well-defined and reusable object-oriented designs.

5.3 Inheritance and Polymorphism: Creating Class Hierarchies

Inheritance

Inheritance is a mechanism that allows you to create new classes based on existing classes. The new class, called[1] the subclass or child class, inherits the properties and methods of the parent class. This promotes code reusability and helps organize complex systems.

Example:

Swift
```
class Animal {
    var name: String

    init(name: String) {
```

```swift
        self.name = name
    }

    func makeSound() {
        print("Generic animal sound")
    }
}

class Dog: Animal {
    override func makeSound() {
        print("Woof!")
    }
}

class Cat: Animal {
    override func makeSound() {
        print("Meow!")
    }
}
```

Polymorphism

Polymorphism allows objects of different classes to be treated as if they were objects of a common superclass. This enables you to write more flexible and generic code.

Method Overriding:

Overriding allows a subclass to provide a specific implementation of a method inherited from its superclass. This is how polymorphism is achieved in Swift.

In the example above, the Dog and Cat classes override the makeSound() method to provide their specific implementations.

Key Points:

Subclassing: Creating a new class based on an existing class.

Method Overriding: Providing a specific implementation of a method in a subclass.

Polymorphism: Treating objects of different classes as if they were objects of a common superclass.

By understanding inheritance and polymorphism, you can create flexible and extensible object-oriented designs.

Chapter 6

Optionals and Error Handling

6.1 Optional Values: Handling the Absence of a Value

In Swift, an optional value is a value that may or may not exist. It is represented by the `Optional<T>` type, where `T` is the type of the value.

Declaring Optional Values:

```
Swift
var optionalString: String?
var optionalInt: Int?
```

Accessing Optional Values:

To access the value of an optional, you must unwrap it. There are two main ways to unwrap an optional:

Optional Binding:

```
Swift

if let unwrappedValue = optionalValue {
    // Use unwrappedValue here
} else {
    // Handle the case where optionalValue is nil
}
```

Forced Unwrapping:
Swift

let unwrappedValue = optionalValue! // Use ! only when you're sure the value exists

Caution: Forced unwrapping can lead to runtime errors if the optional value is `nil`. It's generally recommended to use optional binding to safely unwrap optionals.

Example:

Swift
let optionalName: String? = "Alice"

```
if let name = optionalName {
    print("Hello, \(name)!")
} else {
    print("Name is not available.")
}
```


Nil Coalescing Operator:

The nil-coalescing operator (??) provides a concise way to assign a default value to an optional:

Swift
let defaultName = optionalName ?? "Unknown"
print("Hello, \(defaultName)!")

By understanding optional values and how to safely unwrap them, you can write more robust and error-resistant Swift code.

6.2 Optional Chaining: Safely Accessing Properties and Methods of Optionals

Optional chaining is a powerful feature in Swift that allows you to access properties and call methods on optional values in a safe way. If the optional value is `nil`, the expression will return `nil` instead of causing a runtime error.

Basic Syntax:

```swift
Swift
optionalValue?.property
optionalValue?.method()
```

Example:

```swift
Swift
class Person {
    var name: String?
    var address: Address?
}

class Address {
    var street: String?
}

let person: Person? = Person()
person?.name = "Alice"
person?.address?.street = "123 Main St"

if let street = person?.address?.street {
    print("Street: \(street)")
} else {
    print("Address not available.")
}
```

How it Works:

The expression `person?.address` is evaluated. If `person` is `nil`, the entire expression returns `nil`.

If `person` is not `nil`, the `address` property is accessed. If `address` is `nil`, the expression returns `nil`.

If both `person` and `address` are not `nil`, the `street` property is accessed.

By using optional chaining, you can write more concise and safer code, avoiding potential runtime errors.

6.3 Error Handling: Managing Errors and Exceptions

Error handling is a crucial aspect of writing robust and reliable code. Swift provides a powerful error handling mechanism using `do-catch` blocks.

Basic Syntax:

```
Swift
do {
   // Try to execute code that might throw an error
} catch error {
   // Handle the error
}
```

Throwing Errors:

To signal an error, you can throw an error object of type `Error`.

Swift
```swift
enum MyError: Error {
    case networkError
    case invalidInput
}

func divide(numerator: Int, denominator: Int) throws -> Int {
    if denominator == 0 {
        throw MyError.invalidInput
    }
    return numerator / denominator
}
```

Handling Errors:

Swift
```swift
do {
    let result = try divide(numerator: 10, denominator: 0)
    print(result)
} catch MyError.invalidInput {
    print("Invalid input: denominator cannot be zero.")
} catch {
    print("An unknown error occurred.")
}
```

Key Points:

`do-catch` blocks are used to handle errors.

`throw` keyword is used to signal an error.

`try` keyword is used to indicate a potentially throwing expression.

`catch` blocks are used to handle specific error types or generic errors.

You can propagate errors using `throws` and `rethrows` keywords.

By effectively handling errors, you can create more reliable and user-friendly applications.

Chapter 7

Collections

7.1 Arrays: Storing Ordered Collections of Values

An array is a collection of values, all of the same type, stored in a specific order. You can access individual elements of an array using their index, which starts from 0.

Creating an Array:

```swift
Swift
let numbers = [1, 2, 3, 4, 5]
let names = ["Alice", "Bob", "Charlie"]
```

Accessing Elements:

```swift
Swift
let firstNumber = numbers[0] // Access the first element
let secondName = names[1] // Access the second element
```

Modifying Elements:

```swift
Swift
var mutableNumbers = [1, 2, 3]
mutableNumbers[1] = 10 // Modify the second element
```

Array Properties and Methods:

`count`: Returns the number of elements in the array.

`isEmpty`: Returns `true` if the array is empty, otherwise `false`.

`first`: Returns the first element of the array.

`last`: Returns the last element of the array.

`append(_:)`: Adds an element to the end of the array.

`insert(_:at:)`: Inserts an element at a specific index.

`remove(at:)`: Removes an element at a specific index.

`removeFirst()`: Removes the first element.

`removeLast()`: Removes the last element.

Example:

```Swift
var shoppingList = ["Milk", "Eggs", "Bread"]
shoppingList.append("Butter") // Add "Butter" to the end
shoppingList.insert("Apples", at: 1) // Insert "Apples" at index 1

print(shoppingList.count) // Output: 5
print(shoppingList.first) // Output: Optional("Milk")
print(shoppingList.last) // Output: Optional("Butter")
```

By understanding arrays, you can effectively store and manipulate collections of data in your Swift programs.

7.2 Dictionaries: Storing Key-Value Pairs

A dictionary is an unordered collection of key-value pairs. Each key is unique and associated with a corresponding value.

Creating a Dictionary:

Swift
let ages = ["Alice": 30, "Bob": 25, "Charlie": 35]

Accessing Values:

Swift
let aliceAge = ages["Alice"] // Access the value for the key "Alice"

Modifying Values:

Swift
var mutableAges = ["Alice": 30, "Bob": 25]
mutableAges["Bob"] = 26 // Update the value for the key "Bob"

Adding and Removing Key-Value Pairs:

Swift
mutableAges["David"] = 28 // Add a new key-value pair
mutableAges["Alice"] = nil // Remove the key-value pair for "Alice"

Dictionary Properties and Methods:

`count`: Returns the number of key-value pairs in the dictionary.

`isEmpty`: Returns `true` if the dictionary is empty, otherwise `false`.

`keys`: Returns an array of all keys in the dictionary.

`values`: Returns an array of all values in the dictionary.

`removeValue(forKey:)`: Removes the value for a given key.

Example:

```swift
Swift
var studentGrades = ["Math": 95, "Science": 88, "English": 92]
studentGrades["History"] = 85 // Add a new subject and grade

print(studentGrades.count) // Output: 4
print(studentGrades.keys) // Output: ["Math", "Science", "English", "History"]
print(studentGrades.values) // Output: [95, 88, 92, 85]

studentGrades.removeValue(forKey: "Math") // Remove the "Math" grade
```

By using dictionaries, you can efficiently store and retrieve data based on unique keys, making your code more organized and readable.

7.3 Sets: Storing Unique Values

A set is an unordered collection of unique elements. It's useful for removing duplicates from a collection of values or for checking if a value exists in a collection.

Creating a Set:

```swift
Swift
let numbers = Set([1, 2, 3, 2, 1]) // {1, 2, 3}
let letters = Set(["a", "b", "c", "a"]) // {"a", "b", "c"}
```

Adding Elements:

```swift
Swift
var mutableSet = Set<Int>()
```

```
mutableSet.insert(1)
mutableSet.insert(2)
mutableSet.insert(1) // No effect, as 1 already exists
```

Removing Elements:

Swift
```
mutableSet.remove(2) // Remove the element 2
```

Set Operations:

Union: Combines two sets, removing duplicates.

Swift
```
let set1 = Set([1, 2, 3])
let set2 = Set([2, 3, 4])
let unionSet = set1.union(set2) // {1, 2, 3, 4}
```

Intersection: Finds the common elements between two sets.
Swift
```
let intersectionSet = set1.intersection(set2) // {2, 3}
```

Subtracting: Removes elements from one set that are present in another.

Swift
```
let differenceSet = set1.subtracting(set2) // {1}
```

Symmetric Difference: Combines elements from both sets, excluding common elements.

Swift

let symmetricDifferenceSet = set1.symmetricDifference(set2) // {1, 4}

Key Points:

Sets are unordered, meaning the elements don't have a specific order.

Sets automatically remove duplicates.

Set operations provide powerful tools for working with collections of unique values.

By understanding sets, you can effectively work with unique collections of data in your Swift programs.

Chapter 8

User Interface Design with SwiftUI

8.1 The Basics of SwiftUI: A Declarative Approach to UI Design

SwiftUI is a powerful framework for building user interfaces across all Apple platforms. It uses a declarative approach, meaning you describe what you want the UI to look like, and SwiftUI takes care of the rest.

Key Concepts:

Views:

The fundamental building block of SwiftUI.

Represent UI elements like text, images, buttons, and more.

Defined using a declarative syntax.

State and Data Flow:

SwiftUI uses a state-driven approach to update the UI.

When the state changes, the UI automatically updates.

State can be managed using @State and @ObservedObject properties.

Modifiers:

Modify the appearance and behavior of views.

Chained together to create complex UI layouts.

Examples: `foregroundColor`, `font`, `padding`, `frame`.

Basic Example:

```Swift
import SwiftUI

struct ContentView: View {
    var body: some View {
        Text("Hello, SwiftUI!")
            .font(.largeTitle)
            .padding()
    }
}
```

Breakdown:

`Text("Hello, SwiftUI!")`: Creates a text view with the given text.

`.font(.largeTitle)`: Sets the font size to large title.

`.padding()`: Adds padding around the text.

Creating a Simple UI:

```Swift
struct ContentView: View {
    @State private var count = 0

    var body: some View {
        VStack {
            Text("Count: \(count)")
                .font(.largeTitle)
            Button("Increment") {
                count += 1
```

```
      }
    }
    .padding()
  }
}
```

Key Points:

SwiftUI's declarative syntax makes it easy to build complex UI layouts.

State management is crucial for updating the UI dynamically.

Modifiers allow you to customize the appearance and behavior of views.

By understanding these fundamental concepts, you can start building beautiful and responsive user interfaces with SwiftUI.

8.2 Building User Interfaces: Creating Views, Text, Images, and Other UI Elements

SwiftUI provides a rich set of views and modifiers to create a variety of user interfaces. Here are some common UI elements and how to create them:

Text:

Basic Text:

Swift

```
Text("Hello, SwiftUI!")
```

Customizing Text:

Swift

```
Text("Hello")
    .font(.largeTitle)
    .foregroundColor(.blue)
    .fontWeight(.bold)
```

Images:

Image from Asset Catalog:

Swift

```
Image("myImage")
    .resizable()
    .aspectRatio(contentMode: .fit)
    .frame(width: 200, height: 200)
```

Image from URL:

Swift
```
AsyncImage(url: URL(string: "https://example.com/image.jpg"))
```

Buttons:

Basic Button:

Swift

```
Button("Tap Me") {
    // Button action
}
```

Customizing Button:
Swift

```
Button(action: {
    // Button action
}) {
    Text("Tap Me")
        .foregroundColor(.white)
        .padding()
        .background(.blue)
        .cornerRadius(10)
}
```

Stacks:

VStack: Stacks views vertically.

HStack: Stacks views horizontally.

```
Swift
VStack {
    Text("Hello")
    Image("myImage")
    Button("Tap Me") {
        // Button action
    }
}
```

List:

Simple List:

Swift

```
List {
    Text("Item 1")
    Text("Item 2")
    Text("Item 3")
}
```

List with Data:

Swift

```
List(items: ["Item 1", "Item 2", "Item 3"]) { item in
    Text(item)
}
```

Form:

Simple Form:

Swift

```
Form {
    Section("Personal Information") {
        Text("Name: John Doe")
        Text("Age: 30")
    }
}
```

By combining these basic building blocks and using SwiftUI's declarative syntax, you can create complex and beautiful user interfaces for your iOS and macOS apps.

8.3 Data Flow and State Management: Managing Data and Updating the UI

A key aspect of SwiftUI is its declarative approach to UI development. This involves defining the desired UI state, and SwiftUI takes care of updating the UI whenever the state changes.

State Management

SwiftUI provides two primary ways to manage state:

@State Property Wrapper:

Used for local state within a view.

Changes to the state property trigger a re-render of the view.

Swift

```swift
struct ContentView: View {
   @State private var count = 0

   var body: some View {
      Button("Increment") {
         count += 1
      }
      Text("Count: \(count)")
   }
}
```

@ObservedObject Property Wrapper:
Used for global state that needs to be shared across multiple views.
Requires a class that conforms to the `ObservableObject` protocol.

```swift
Swift
class Counter: ObservableObject {
    @Published var count = 0
}

struct ContentView: View {
    @ObservedObject var counter = Counter()

    var body: some View {
        Button("Increment") {
            counter.count += 1
        }
        Text("Count: \(counter.count)")
    }
}
```

Data Flow:

SwiftUI uses a unidirectional data flow model, meaning data flows from the source of truth (your model) to the views. This helps maintain a clear and predictable state management system.

Key Points:

Use @State for simple state management within a view.

Use @ObservedObject for complex state that needs to be shared across multiple views.

Always update the state in a predictable and efficient manner.Use SwiftUI's built-in mechanisms for data flow to ensure a clean and maintainable architecture.

By understanding data flow and state management, you can create dynamic and responsive user interfaces in SwiftUI.

Chapter 9

App Architecture

9.1 Model-View-Controller (MVC) Design Pattern: Structuring Your App for Maintainability

The Model-View-Controller (MVC) design pattern is a popular architectural pattern used to structure software applications. It divides an application into three interconnected parts:

Model: Represents the data and business logic of the application.

View: Defines the visual presentation of the data.

Controller: Handles user interaction and updates the model and view.

In SwiftUI:

While SwiftUI doesn't strictly enforce the MVC pattern, it aligns well with its principles.

Model: Often represented by plain Swift structs or classes that hold data.

View: SwiftUI views themselves, defining the UI layout and presentation.

Controller: Implicitly handled by SwiftUI's data flow and state management mechanisms.

Example:

```swift
Swift
// Model
struct User {
    var name: String
    var age: Int
}

// View
struct UserView: View {
    @State private var user = User(name: "Alice", age: 30)

    var body: some View {
        VStack {
            Text("Name: \(user.name)")
            Text("Age: \(user.age)")
            Button("Update Age") {
                user.age += 1
            }
        }
    }
}
```

Key Benefits of MVC:

Separation of Concerns: Clear separation of data, presentation, and logic.

Reusability: Reusable components and easier testing.

Maintainability: Easier to understand, modify, and test.

Flexibility: Adaptable to changes in requirements.

By understanding and applying the MVC pattern, you can create well-structured, maintainable, and scalable SwiftUI applications.

9.2 Dependency Injection: Managing Dependencies Between Components

Dependency injection is a technique for managing dependencies between software components. It involves providing the dependencies to a component rather than the component creating them itself. This promotes loose coupling and makes your code more modular and testable.

Types of Dependency Injection:

Property Injection:

Dependencies are injected as properties of a class.

Swift

```
class MyClass {
   let dependency: DependencyType

   init(dependency: DependencyType) {
      self.dependency = dependency
   }
}
```

Method Injection:

Dependencies are injected as parameters to a method.

```Swift
class MyClass {
    func doSomething(dependency: DependencyType) {
        // Use dependency
    }
}
```

Constructor Injection:

Dependencies are injected through the class's initializer.

```Swift
class MyClass {
    let dependency: DependencyType

    init(dependency: DependencyType) {
        self.dependency = dependency
    }
}
```

Benefits of Dependency Injection:

Testability: Easily mock dependencies for unit testing.

Flexibility: Components can be easily replaced or modified.

Loose Coupling: Reduces tight coupling between components.

Reusability: Components can be reused in different contexts.

In SwiftUI:

While SwiftUI doesn't explicitly require dependency injection, you can use it to manage complex dependencies, especially in large-scale applications. For example, you can inject services, data sources, or other dependencies into your views and view models.

By understanding dependency injection, you can create more modular, testable, and maintainable SwiftUI applications.

9.3 Testing Your App: Writing Unit and UI Tests

Testing is a crucial part of software development to ensure quality and reliability. Swift and Xcode provide powerful tools for writing unit tests and UI tests.

Unit Tests:

Unit tests focus on testing individual units of code, such as functions and methods. They help ensure that each component works as expected.

Writing Unit Tests:

Create a Test Target: Add a new test target to your Xcode project.

Write Test Cases: Create test cases that test different scenarios and edge cases.

Use XCTest Assertions: Verify the expected behavior of your code using assertions like XCTAssertEqual, XCTAssertTrue, and XCTAssertFalse.

Example:

```
Swift
import XCTest
@testable import MyProject
```

```swift
class MyFunctionTests: XCTestCase {
    func testMyFunction() {
        let result = myFunction(input: 5)
        XCTAssertEqual(result, 10)
    }
}
```

UI Tests:

UI tests simulate user interactions with your app's UI. They help ensure that the UI works as expected and that user interactions are handled correctly.

Writing UI Tests:

Create a UI Test Target: Add a new UI test target to your Xcode project.

Record Interactions: Use the Xcode UI Testing Recorder to record user interactions with your app.

Write Test Cases: Customize the recorded tests and add assertions to verify the expected behavior.

Example:

```swift
Swift
import XCTest

class MyUITests: XCTestCase {
    func testLogin() {
        let app = XCUIApplication()
        app.launch()

        // ... (Record user interactions to log in)
```

```
    XCTAssertTrue(app.staticTexts["Welcome"].exists)
  }
}
```

Key Points:

Write clear and concise test cases.

Cover a wide range of scenarios, including edge cases and error conditions.

Run tests regularly to catch regressions early.

Use test-driven development (TDD) to write tests before writing code.

By writing comprehensive unit and UI tests, you can improve the quality and reliability of your Swift applications.

Chapter 10

Advanced Topics

10.1 Core Data: Storing and Managing Persistent Data

Core Data is a powerful framework provided by Apple for managing persistent data in iOS, macOS, watchOS, and tvOS applications. It allows you to create data models, store data in a persistent store, and retrieve data as needed.

Key Concepts:

Entity: Represents a type of data, similar to a class in object-oriented programming.

Attribute: A property of an entity, such as a name, age, or address.

Relationship: A connection between two entities, such as a one-to-one, one-to-many, or many-to-many relationship.

Managed Object Context: An object that manages a set of managed objects and interacts with the persistent store.

Persistent Store Coordinator: Coordinates access to persistent stores, such as SQLite databases.

Basic Steps to Use Core Data:

Create a Data Model:

Design your data model using the Core Data editor in Xcode.

Define entities, attributes, and relationships.

Create a Managed Object Context:

Initialize a `NSManagedObjectContext` to manage data.

Create and Save Managed Objects:

Create instances of managed objects and set their properties.

Save the context to persist the changes.

Fetch and Update Managed Objects:

Use `NSFetchRequest` to fetch managed objects based on specific criteria.

Update the properties of fetched objects and save the context.

Delete Managed Objects:

Delete managed objects using the `delete(_:)` method of the managed object context.

Example:

```swift
Swift
// Create a managed object context
let context = persistentContainer.viewContext

// Create a new person entity
let person = Person(context: context)
person.name = "Alice"
person.age = 30

// Save the context
do {
    try context.save()
} catch {
```

```
    // Handle error
}

// Fetch people
let        fetchRequest:        NSFetchRequest<Person>        =
Person.fetchRequest()
let people = try context.fetch(fetchRequest)

// Update a person
people[0].age = 31
try context.save()
```

By understanding Core Data's core concepts and following best practices, you can effectively manage persistent data in your iOS and macOS applications.

10.2 Networking: Making Network Requests and Handling Responses

Networking is essential for modern applications, allowing them to communicate with servers and retrieve or send data. Swift provides several ways to make network requests, including:

1. URLSession:

A powerful and flexible framework for making network requests.

You can use it to make GET, POST, PUT, DELETE, and other types of requests.

Example:

```
Swift
let url = URL(string: "https://api.example.com/data")!
```

```swift
let task = URLSession.shared.dataTask(with: url) { data, response,
error in
    if let error = error {
        print("Error: \(error)")
        return
    }

    guard let data = data else {
        print("No data received")
        return
    }

    if let jsonResult = try? JSONSerialization.jsonObject(with: data,
options: []) as? [String: Any] {
        print(jsonResult)
    }
}
task.resume()
```

2. URLSession with Combine:

Combines URLSession with the Combine framework for a more declarative and functional approach.

Example:

```swift
Swift
let url = URL(string: "https://api.example.com/data")!
URLSession.shared.dataTaskPublisher(for: url)
    .map { data, response in
        return data
    }
    .receive(on: DispatchQueue.main)
    .sink { completion in
        if case let .failure(error) = completion {
```

```
        print("Error: \(error)")
    }
  } receiveValue: { data in
        if let jsonResult = try? JSONSerialization.jsonObject(with:
data, options: []) as? [String: Any] {
        print(jsonResult)
    }
  }
  .store(in: &cancellables)
```

3. Third-Party Libraries:

Many third-party libraries simplify network requests and provide additional features.

Popular libraries include Alamofire, Moya, and Combine.

Key Points:

Error Handling: Always handle potential errors, such as network errors, JSON parsing errors, and server errors.

Asynchronous Operations: Use asynchronous techniques like `URLSession.shared.dataTask` or Combine to avoid blocking the main thread.

JSON Parsing: Use `JSONSerialization` or a library like SwiftyJSON to parse JSON data.

Security: Consider using HTTPS to encrypt communication and protect user data.

Rate Limiting: Respect server rate limits to avoid being blocked.

By understanding these concepts and using the appropriate tools, you can effectively make network requests and handle responses in your Swift applications.

10.3 Grand Central Dispatch and Operation Queues: Performing Asynchronous Tasks

Grand Central Dispatch (GCD) and Operation Queues are powerful tools for managing asynchronous tasks in iOS and macOS applications. They allow you to perform background tasks without blocking the main thread, ensuring smooth user experience.

Grand Central Dispatch (GCD):

GCD provides a simple and efficient way to execute tasks concurrently. It uses a queue-based system to manage tasks.

Serial Queue: Executes tasks one at a time, in the order they are added to the queue.

Concurrent Queue: Executes tasks concurrently, as long as the system resources allow.

Example:

```Swift
DispatchQueue.global(qos: .background).async {
    // Perform a long-running task
    let result = performLongRunningTask()

    DispatchQueue.main.async {
        // Update the UI with the result
        updateUI(with: result)
    }
}
```

Operation Queues:

Operation Queues provide a more object-oriented approach to managing asynchronous tasks. They offer additional features like dependencies, priorities, and cancellation.

Example:

```
Swift
let queue = OperationQueue()

let operation1 = BlockOperation {
    // Perform task 1
}

let operation2 = BlockOperation {
    // Perform task 2
}

operation2.addDependency(operation1)

queue.addOperations([operation1, operation2], waitUntilFinished:
true)
```

Key Points:

Main Thread: The main thread is responsible for updating the UI. Avoid blocking it with long-running tasks.

Background Threads: Use background threads (e.g., GCD or Operation Queues) to perform time-consuming tasks.

Asynchronous Programming: Use asynchronous techniques to prevent blocking the main thread.

Callback Blocks: Use callback blocks to handle the completion of asynchronous tasks.

Combine Framework: Combine provides a declarative and functional approach to asynchronous programming.

By effectively using GCD and Operation Queues, you can create responsive and efficient iOS and macOS applications.

www.ingramcontent.com/pod-product-compliance
Lightning Source LLC
LaVergne TN
LVHW051741050326
832903LV00023B/1042